CAST IRON

This book provides a visual feast through the eyes of the exceptional photographer John Gay. As Gavin Stamp says in his Introduction 'cast iron is arguably the most varied, the most useful, the most decorative element in the architecture of the last two centuries', and John Gay shows that it can also be visually the most exciting.

Cast iron is everywhere although we often take it for granted. It soars above us holding up railway station roofs, it has the delicacy of lace in the great conservatories at Kew Gardens and the Botanic Gardens in Glasgow, and elephantine strength in the Albert Dock in Liverpool. Verandahs, balconies, gates and railings offer 'bursts of exquisite detail' and humour is often there as with the camel and sphinx ornamental seats on the Thames Embankment.

John Gay's superb photographs together with Gavin Stamp's lively and informative introduction offer a new look at this underrated element in architecture.

Other books of photographs by John Gay include *Highgate Cemetery: Victorian Valhalla* (John Murray), *London Observed* (Michael Joseph), *Prospect of Hampstead and Highgate* (Highgate Press) and *London's Historic Railway Stations* with John Betjeman (John Murray).

JOHN MURRAY

CAST

Architecture and Ornament,

Function and Fantasy

IRON

Photographed by JOHN GAY

Introduced by Gavin Stamp

Photographs © John Gay 1985
Introduction © Gavin Stamp 1985

First published 1985
by John Murray (Publishers) Ltd
50 Albemarle Street, London W1X 4BD

Printed and bound in Great Britain
by Butler & Tanner Ltd, Frome and London

British Library CIP Data
Gay, John, *1909–*
Cast iron: architecture & ornament,
function & fantasy.
1. Ironwork—Pictorial works
2. Cast-iron—Pictorial works
I. Title   739'.4   NK8205
ISBN 0-7195-4230-8

CONTENTS

INTRODUCTION
GAVIN STAMP

ORNAMENT IS NO CRIME, whatever Adolf Loos may have said. And there is no better way of achieving economical, durable, functional ornament, or indeed of combining function and ornament together, than by using cast iron. Yet cast iron has had a bad press. For most of its life it has been condemned by architectural theorists and purists, who have considered the repetition of detail by casting somehow vulgar compared with the individual craftsmanship required in the working of wrought iron.

Cast iron in architecture began at a disadvantage. Probably the first example of it in England was the railings around St Paul's Cathedral, made in 1710-14 by Richard Jones in the Sussex Weald and which still largely survive. Unfortunately they were installed against the wishes of Sir Christopher Wren, who therefore criticised them and argued for a wrought iron fence instead. In the mid-nineteenth century, cast iron was condemned by the earnest Gothic Revivalists precisely because it was cast. They took their lead from Ruskin who, in the *Seven Lamps of Architecture* in 1849, maintained that 'No ornaments ... are so cold, clumsy and vulgar, so essentially incapable of a fine line or shadow, as those of cast iron; and while, on the score of truth, we can hardly allege any thing against them, since they are always distinguishable, at a glance, from wrought and hammered work, and stand only for what they are, yet I feel very strongly that there is no hope of the progress of the arts of any nation which indulges in these vulgar and cheap substitutes for real decoration.'

Can any adjectives be more damning, in snobbish, moralistic Britain, than 'vulgar and cheap'? Cast ironwork, whether ornamental or constructional, became hopelessly associated with industry, with mass production, with popular taste, with everything the Gothic Revival and its Arts and Crafts successors were standing against. Cast iron seems the Cinderella of architecture. Yet it is *everywhere* and we simply could not do without it, whether in town or country. It holds up the roofs of railway stations and markets; it is made into bridges; it conveys information in the form of street signs and notices; it is the basic material of so much that is essential – so essential that we take it for granted. Cast iron is arguably the most varied, the most useful, the most decorative element in the architecture of the last two centuries. Take it away and we are all the poorer, our streets the more barren, our buildings the more stark.

To see the wonders of cast iron, to appreciate its ubiquity and usefulness, you must have an eye like the lens of John Gay's camera. And you will be a danger to yourself and to others, for if you walk through the streets looking at all the details so decoratively made in cast iron you will be looking everywhere but where you are going. (This is why the real architectural enthusiast always walks and must *never* be allowed to drive or bicycle.) Look up, and you will see balconies and hanging signs and fanlights over doors; look to one side and you will see railings with decorative finials, delighting the eye and, at the same time, preventing you from plunging down into chasms; look to the other and you may see the beauty of old street furniture made of cast iron: lamp posts, pillar boxes and telephone kiosks. Or look down at your feet and you may see the round coal-hole covers, each different, each decorative, each bearing the name of its maker.

But there is more. There are the bollards at street corners, sometimes in the shape of a gun with the initials of the parish and the date cast in the iron, sometimes chamfered and fluted horizontally, bearing the monogram of King William IV; there are ornamental gates, either on public buildings or announcing the entrance to a public park, and the park may well contain ornamental seats of iron – though probably not as exotic as those which stand near the Dolphin lamps – also of cast iron – on the Victoria Embankment, with supporting ends shaped like camels or sphinxes [49, 50]*. And then there are the notices: 'Great Northern Railway. Penalty for Trespassing upon the Railway ...' &c., or those bearing street names. Why, in the era of cast iron, was lettering so much more distinguished than today, when signs are of pressed alloy or the legend is conveyed by ugly, badly proportioned lower-case letters made from transfers? Does cast iron impose a discipline, or did it flourish at a high point in civilisation, when men knew how to letter, to design and to embellish as if by instinct?

And then there is the cast iron inside the home: grates, radiators, doorstops. The list of possibilities seems endless. This versatility comes from the essential simplicity of the process. The iron is cast, in moulds, and so a particular pattern of railing, or column, can be produced in large numbers, identically, at comparatively low prices. Low, that is, compared with wrought iron, in which each finial, each spiral and curlicue must be hammered out by the hand of the blacksmith.

It is important to distinguish between wrought and cast iron. Mediaeval ironwork was wrought, or cut from sheet metal. Wrought iron is more malleable; cast iron, containing more impurities, is strong but brittle; it is easily shattered but, in the form of columns, will bear immense loads. As such, cast iron only really came into its own in the Industrial Revolution and in the

* The numbers in brackets in the text refer to the photographs

nineteenth century; its strength permitted the construction of iron buildings while its ability to be moulded allowed those buildings to be ornamented and embellished. Before the eighteenth century its use was largely for cannon balls, guns and firebacks – those handsome and functional features of large chimney-pieces which can be so charmingly decorative.

★   ★   ★

Cast iron began to be used in architecture in the early eighteenth century. At first, much of it imitated wrought iron, in particular the designs illustrated in *A New Booke of Drawings* published by Jean Tijou in 1693. But the railings around St Paul's which Wren disliked and those designed by Gibbs in the 1720s to protect St Martin's in the Fields and the Senate House in Cambridge show an appreciation of the nature of the material, for, in the latter, uprights of wrought iron alternate with splendidly fat and curvaceous balusters of cast iron, topped with carefully shaped finials. But such railings were special jobs, especially designed for public buildings. More typical and much more common are the railings and other iron elements designed for the tens of thousands of houses constructed during the building booms of the eighteenth and early nineteenth centuries. Here the demand was for mass production.

Cast iron was peculiarly appropriate to Georgian architecture, for it actually needed to be repetitive and to fit in precisely defined positions. Georgian streets depended upon proportion and repetition for effect and the same system governed the design of houses, whether grand or humble. The quality of Georgian architecture – which the Victorians found so desperately boring – was beautifully defined by Robert Byron: 'Its reserve and dislike of outward show, its reliance on the virtue and dignity of proportions only, and its rare bursts of exquisite detail, all express as no other style has ever done that indifference to self-advertisement, that quiet assumption of our own worth, and that sudden vein of lyric affection, which have given us our part in civilisation.'

So cast iron supplanted wrought iron, and its ascendancy coincided with the Industrial Revolution and the understanding of mass production. The success of cast iron in architecture therefore depended on standardisation combined with immense decorative flexibility to produce those 'rare bursts of exquisite detail'. This success depended on the existence of firms which came to specialise in cast iron decorative elements and on the availability of pattern books. At first the patterns were just concerned with motifs that were fashionable. The publication of *The Works in Architecture by Robert and James Adam* in the 1770s promoted the Adam Brothers and allowed their light, decorative Neo-Classical style to be imitated the world over. It also allowed their characteristic motifs to be mass produced in cast iron so that, for the next half century, their balcony design with an anthemion pattern became one of the commonest to be applied to new houses.

Inspired by the Adams' came other pattern books, specifically for cast iron-work. One example is a book of the 1790s by I. and J. Taylor entitled *Ornamental Iron Work, or Designs in the Present Taste, for Fan-Lights, Stair-case railing, Window-guard-irons, Lamp-irons, Palisades, & Gates. With a Scheme for adjusting Designs with facility and accuracy to any slope*, which covers just about everything the builder might need. More pattern books appeared in the first few decades of the nineteenth century, to supply details for the ubiquitous and elegant standardised Regency architecture associated with the Metropolitan Improvements of John Nash. Without cast iron, indeed, the achievement of Nash and his contemporaries would not have been possible.

In 1823 the architect and antiquarian L. N. Cottingham published *The Ornamental Metal Workers' Director*. The preface is most revealing, as 'The extensive application of metal, in securing, decorating, and furnishing every class of building, from the superb palace of the monarch to the social villa of the retired citizen, renders any apology for introducing a Work of this description unnecessary.' Cast iron was a social leveller; indeed it brought ornament to almost everybody. 'The great improvement that has taken place in our Brass and Iron Foundries within these last twenty years, has elevated this branch of English manufacture far above that of every other country, and raised the articles which were formerly considered as merely gross and ponderous, into the scale of ornamental embellishment, in which utility and security are united with the lightness and elegance of classical design ...'

The range of applicability of cast iron was now extended: 'Many of the subjects introduced in this Work have been executed from the designs of the most eminent artists; and those composed by the Author are from the best specimens of antique ornament, consisting of Entrance Gates to public buildings, parks, gardens, &c. Verandas, Fences: Balcony, Area, and Window Guards; Balustrades and Newels for staircases and galleries; Fanlights, Lamps and Brackets for entrance doors; Street Lamps; grand Stands for gas-lights; Tripods, Candelabra, Candlesticks, Chandeliers; Vases and Pedestals; Hot-air stoves for churches, chapels, and public offices; elegant Stoves and Fenders for drawing rooms, &c., &c. serviceable for ladies and gentlemen to select from,

10

and equally so to the furnishing Ironmonger.' The following year this work was expanded as *The Smith and Founder's Director*. A similarly useful pattern book was Henry Shaw's *Examples of Ornamental Metal Work*, published in 1836 and illustrating designs by many different architects and artists.

Later in the nineteenth century, pattern books become catalogues, issued by a particular manufacturer. These catalogues are invaluable in identifying and dating cast ironwork both in Britain and abroad, and it is sad that comparatively few have been preserved, for without them we lack documentation about so characteristic and so widespread an aspect of Victorian architecture. The firms which made cast iron products were numerous, as may be seen by observating the trademarks on columns or grates, radiators or bollards. Very few of these firms survive today. A particularly important and distinguished firm was the Carron Company, established in 1759 near Falkirk and which, sadly, only finally went out of business in 1983. At first the Carron Company specialised in cannon and ordnance, but soon their range expanded. Their goods were of high quality and thoroughly fashionable in design. John Adam was a director and the Adams used the firm's products, so Carron grates or railings were sophisticated in form and Neo-Classical in style. The Carron Company was the Wedgwood of cast iron.

More typical of the Victorian Age is a firm like Walter Macfarlane & Co. of Glasgow, a firm whose catalogues went all over the world and particularly to different parts of the British Empire. The ubiquity of cast iron is not merely British; it is Imperial. Balconies, and bandstands, ornamental gates and fountains, indeed whole prefabricated buildings, are to be found, bearing the Macfarlane trademark, in Bombay and Calcutta, Melbourne and Adelaide, Cape Town and Durban. Items were ordered from the Macfarlane or other catalogues and shipped out; later they were imitated by independent foundries established in the Colonies. If there was an Imperial British style, it was not Classical or Gothic, or, indeed, in any definite architectural style, for all over the Empire buildings were eclectic and various. The only continuity, the only consistent element found in India and Australia, South Africa and the West Indies is the presence of cast iron products: verandahs, balconies, gates and railings, exported by British (usually Scottish) firms. It is not too far fetched to claim that cast iron architectural elements bound the British Empire together. They are still what makes the former parts of the Empire distinctive and recognisable.

But by the time that cast iron was being exported all over the world, its architectural applications were going out of fashion back home. The real Age of cast iron in Britain was the Regency and the first half of Victoria's reign. In domestic architecture, the Regency developed the use of iron decoration established by the Georgians. Those 'rare bursts of exquisite detail' on terraced houses were still of iron. Sometimes, as with the lamp brackets on the more expensive houses, the detail was of wrought iron, but most of it was cast. Because the typical house was raised up on a basement, with cellars beneath the pavement, there was need for a considerable amount of iron: a cover for the coal hole and railings to protect the 'area' – the chasm between pavement and basement wall – and to guard and define the steps rising up to the front door. Even such railings gave ample scope for elaboration, for the uprights could end as spear-heads or more extravagant shapes like fleurs-de-lys, while the corners were turned with an urn or pineapple. Later, the uprights themselves could be extravagantly ornamental and not just square in section. Then, thanks to the fashion set by the Adam Brothers, there was the fanlight above the front door, that semi-circular glazed area which, even on poorer houses, was filled by a standard mass-produced ornamental pattern of glazing achieved often with cast iron, but sometimes with the help of wrought iron and lead. The shape of a fan was the basic form, but this could be developed into extravagant and fanciful patterns.

However, the principal area for 'exquisite detail' was on the first floor, or *piano nobile*, which, in the Italian manner, was the principal floor in Regency as with Georgian houses. The large front windows, often reaching to the floor, needed to be protected, so a balcony of cast iron was fixed to the façade. Sometimes there was one small balcony to each window, sometimes it stretched right across the façade, but in each case it was manufactured in cast iron and given an elegant decorative pattern, governed by roundels, ovals, or the large scrolls of the anthemion favoured by the Adams. To achieve a finer, filigree effect, open borders could be of Greek key, or wave patterns, or any other form which could be achieved in the medium of cast iron.

The effect of a street of balconies seen in perspective is splendid, especially if they are supported on ornamental brackets. Even better if the balcony fronts are not straight but curved in section; better still if the balcony is developed upwards, with thin vertical supports holding up a metal canopy or roof. This is a form of façade treatment which seems especially characteristic of the Regency and which was particularly favoured, not in central London, but in more countrified locations, like Hampstead, or in spas and seaside resorts, like Cheltenham or Brighton. The most delicate structures, almost covering the façade,

12

could be achieved with sections of cast iron manufacture. At the other end of the social scale, even a humble little house could have a simple cast iron window guard to put flower pots behind, and this was given a decorative flourish with Greek, or floral detail. Cast iron could make all architecture interesting.

In the reign of the greatest George, from the artistic point of view – the Prince Regent, George IV – the forms of cast iron architectural decoration became much less imitative of the delicacy of wrought iron and more expressive of the nature of the heavy, brittle, fluid material. Railings, in particular, became more massive and dense, more decorative and yet more solid. This can be seen in the grander railings and palisades on public buildings of the Greek Revival, such as those put around the British Museum by Smirke or in front of Apsley House for the Iron Duke by Benjamin Dean Wyatt. But, as the Victorians would later complain, nothing was wholly true and honest, for these last railings, like those all over London, were painted a dusty pale green to look like weathered bronze, just as the ubiquitous stucco was originally painted – complete with joints – to imitate fashionable Bath stone.

These same decades saw a massive expansion of the use of cast iron, exploiting not only its mass productive and decorative potential but also its constructive utility. Bridges and whole buildings were made of cast iron, producing structures which were elegant as well as strong. The first cast iron bridge is that made by Abraham Darby in 1778 at the eponymous Ironbridge, or Coalbrookdale, the centre of iron manufacture. By the early years of the nineteenth century, the great Telford was constructing aqueducts and bridges of iron. That over the Conway at Bettws-y-Coed combined the structural and decorative characteristics of the medium in a single elegant arch, for its filigree structure is embellished with heraldic flowers, given a decorative light handrail and bears the inscription, in bold, well-proportioned lettering, 'This Arch was constructed in the same year that the Battle of Waterloo was fought.'

More and more masonry buildings came to use cast iron construction. Often the iron columns were visible and, therefore, carefully proportioned as with those supporting galleries in churches. The proportions varied greatly. In the kitchen of the Brighton Pavilion, Nash supported the ceiling on thin shafts of iron which, with the help of iron leaves, masquerade as palm trees, while in the St Katherine's Dock, Telford supported his warehouses on suitably massive and fat Tuscan columns of iron. Similar brutal, Neo-Classical cast iron columns support the arcades of the splendid Albert Dock in Liverpool of the 1840s [30], where the floors were also supported on iron joists and columns, and even the windows – as in many industrial buildings – were made of cast iron, with frame and glazing bars cast all in one piece.

The most famous iron buildings, of course, are those purely of iron and glass; light, elegant, decorative structures with beautiful curved surfaces which seem almost to defy gravity and float like glass bubbles. The use of such structures was limited, but precise. They made magnificent conservatories for the exotic plants which the Early Victorians enthusiastically cultivated. Belfast and Glasgow [27, 29] each boast magnificent palm houses, but the finest of all is surely that at Kew, designed by Richard Turner and Decimus Burton in a mixture of cast and wrought iron and erected in 1844–48. Curved shape is almost everything, but even the cast iron brackets across the clerestory are given Greek motifs while the visitor climbs to the exotic upper levels by functional yet ornamental iron spiral staircases.

The famous cast iron structures by Paxton are sadly no longer with us. The Great Stove at Chatsworth was deliberately destroyed with dynamite; the Crystal Palace accidentally by fire. The Crystal Palace showed the possibilities of prefabricated structures, for it was made of standard cast iron sections bolted together (actually, in the original 1851 structure, there was wrought iron and even *wood* in it as well). Historians complain that the Victorians never exploited the functional potential of the Crystal Palace technology but were obsessed instead with various architectural styles. Such historians ignore the fact that such iron structures had limited uses. They made admirable conservatories and exhibition halls, adequate railway stations and market halls, but were less satisfactory as houses, churches or offices. It is possible to find whole cast iron façades in Glasgow but not in London. This is not because Londoners were less advanced or forward-looking but simply because the exposure of iron construction was illegal under the London Building Acts. In a fire, cast iron is very dangerous: the water from a fireman's hose will shatter the hot iron. In London, therefore, iron supports had to be clad in masonry.

Indeed, the most successful buildings were often a combination of cast iron and masonry. The masonry provided security and insulation; the cast iron allowed a light economical structure which was also strong and decorative. This last element was essential, especially in a type of building not usually associated with new technology. In Liverpool, the architect and antiquarian Thomas Rickman – who coined the terms 'E.E.', 'Dec.' and 'Perp.' – combined with the local ironmaster John Cragg to design not only houses full of cast iron but two churches as well. These – St George's, Everton [20], and St Michael-in-the-

14

Hamlet, Toxteth [21]; both of the early 1810s – are delightful buildings, even though Rickman complained that 'His [Cragg's] ironwork is too stiff in his head to bend to any beauty.' Gothic shafts of cast iron support first galleries and then delicate open iron spandrils which form the arcades and the roof supports. Iron was as suitable to Gothic tracery as it was to Greek anthemions and palmettes; in Liverpool even the church windows are of cast iron.

Ruskin thoroughly disapproved of iron churches, yet he himself was involved in a building of masonry and iron which is not dissimilar to Rickman's Liverpool churches. This is the Oxford Museum [18,19], in which the external walls of Venetian Gothic, designed by Deane & Woodward, conceal an interior court which is roofed and lit by a fantastic structure of iron and glass. Even in the moralistic 1850s iron could be Gothic. Thin shafts of iron support decorated curving ribs and filigree spandrils to create an effect which not only harmonises with the surrounding masonry arcades but which also seems in sympathy with the spiky skeletons of the prehistoric animals beneath.

There is one significant difference between Rickman's Gothic columns and Deane & Woodward's: the latter have proper capitals, with leaves curling under the abacus. Here, they are probably of wrought iron, as each is different and very delicate, but cast iron Gothic capitals could also be made and these provided the authentic decorative touch which the Victorians demanded, even on their utilitarian buildings. Market halls and, above all, railway stations were essentially undecorated structures of iron, but if the roofs were supported on columns, those columns had decorative capitals bolted to the cylindrical shafts. Sometimes, as at Liverpool Street Station [36], the bolts fixing the cast sections have been allowed to rust so that the leafy, foliated iron capitals have fallen off or been taken down, leaving the columns with a more severe geometrical profile than the designers intended. But even here the required delicacy and decoration is given by the cast iron spandrils above which support the main girders, for each is pierced to leave an intricate silhouette of roundels, tendrils and curlicues. And what is true of the big termini is also true of the little suburban or country stations. The platform canopy with its wooden frilly bargeboards (if British Rail have not yet modernised it) is supported on iron columns, with capitals [13,14], and on pierced iron spandrils.

The Victorians were prepared to do extraordinary things with iron. Sadly, one of the best iron structures was wickedly demolished in 1962. This was Bunning's Coal Exchange in the City, whose stuccoed exterior encased a great iron and glass rotunda, with floor after floor of galleries and the iron moulded into fantastic shapes and made to look like coils of rope. The Coal Exchange has gone, but there is still much good ironwork in the City of London to demonstrate how the Victorians exploited the possibilities of cast iron to the full. If Georgian and Regency cast ironwork was delicate and precise, Victorian cast iron is heavy and intricate. This can be seen in Smithfield Market [34, 35] where, in the 1860s, the City Architect, Horace Jones, designed a mixed masonry, wood and iron structure with richly ornamental iron brackets, spandrils and gates. Then there is William Hayward's Holborn Viaduct [39] of the same decade, in which heavy arched girders, pierced and decorated with heraldry and foliated ornament, sit on top of massive granite columns.

Almost anything could be made of cast iron, even prefabricated churches, or 'tin tabernacles', which were went to the Colonies and were soon found to be useless as the congregations roasted in them under the Tropical sun. More sensible were radiators at home, with iron surfaces moulded and pierced to give out greater heat and to look all the more decorative. There is no better way of heating cathedrals than those magnificent coal stoves with radiating fins, topped with a cast iron crown and proudly bearing the legend, in cast Lombardic lettering. 'Gurney's Patent. London Ventilating and Warming Co.' Seats could be made of iron and ornamental gas lamps of iron, like the splendid Dolphin lamps [53] by Timothy Butler which sit on the granite parapet wall of Bazalgette's Victoria Embankment. These were cast with the date of manufacture, so, where the design has subsequently been repeated, as in front of the County Hall in Edwardian times, it is possible easily to date each section of the Thames Embankment. There are even tombstones of cast iron [83], though few Victorians were quite as ferromaniac as the famous ironmaster, John Wilkinson, who made iron coffins and had a 20-ton cast iron obelisk raised to his memory at Lindale, Lancashire, when he died in 1808.

Sadly, the Age of Cast Iron hardly outlived the Age of Victoria. By the 1880s it is clear that cast iron decoration was being dogged by the fatal accusation of vulgarity. Architects in the narrow mainstream of the Gothic Revival and the Arts and Crafts movement hardly ever used it: it was tainted both with the moralistic accusation of untruthfulness; even worse, it was a product of the industrial age and industry was something which Ruskin and Morris turned their backs on. Pugin, prophet and polemicist of the Gothic Revival, complained that 'cast iron is a deception; it is seldom or never left as iron, it is disguised by paint, either as stone, wood, or marble,' and the title page of his notorious *Contrasts* of 1836 has a satirical advertisement for 'Cast Iron Tracery Caps.

16

Gothic Verandas. Tudor Railings and Norman Gothic' as part of his 'Temple of Taste, and Architectural Repository.' Gilbert Scott was rare among Goths in being prepared to experiment with what he called 'architecturalizing cast-iron beams'. In this he enjoyed a considerable degree of success, as may be seen in St Pancras Station, but his contemporaries, like G.E. Street, avoided cast iron and only used wrought or sheet iron in the mediaeval manner.

In the domestic architecture, the 'Queen Anne' style of Norman Shaw had no use for decorative iron and, besides, the typical Late Victorian house had less scope for cast ironwork compared with the Georgian house. There was no area, so railings were not required and, besides, a brick wall and wooden fence was preferred, while the affection for the bay-window abolished the necessity for the balcony. Only surrounding public buildings and blocks of flats or tenements are cast iron railings to be found. Edwardian examples may be touched by *l'art nouveau* and have the uprights relieved by decorative supports which project above the horizontal bar.

The Modern Movement also had no use for decorative iron, but its own austerity was even less popular than Victorian vulgarity. Paradoxically, perhaps, in the 1930s the Modern style was only really tolerated in the one place where the cast iron and vulgar had always been acceptable, even necessary – the seaside. In the late Victorian and Edwardian decades, decorative cast ironwork was either exported or erected along seaside promenades. One of the best examples of festive, ebullient cast ironwork is to be found at Brighton [46] where, in the 1880s, John Every (Lewes) Ltd. cast trellis-like spandrils, railings, ornamental columns and lace-like panels for eaves and roof ridges to make bandstands, shelters and the long covered arcade along Madeira Drive. This has been called 'cake-icing ironwork'. It is absolutely right for the seaside and, in its vaguely Oriental style, is reminiscent of *jalis* or Indian pierced stone screens, and so responds to the masterpiece of cake-icing architecture: Nash's fantastic Royal Pavilion [15] – itself partly constructed of decorative cast iron.

★   ★   ★

Cast iron can be made in any style: Indian, Moorish, Greek, Gothic; it can be big and bold or delicate, filigree and lacy. It is strong and light, and, for comparatively little cost, can add that touch of visual interest and delight which can redeem the dullest, most banal buildings. And the forms it makes are practical and useful. How sad it is, therefore, that so little use is made of decorative cast iron today: its revived use might increase the popularity of the

17

various 'Post–Modern' styles which have arisen to supplant the inhuman aridity of so much modern architecture. Perhaps it need not be of cast iron but cast aluminium or some alloy such as is used in modern reproductions of those heavy ornamental Victorian pub tables. It is the decorativeness which matters.

How barren our streets would be if all the cast iron decoration were to be removed. Many people do not notice how much visual delight there is in their ordinary surroundings, how much decoration there is in iron on all sides; but if it was taken away they would sense a loss. Ruskin, so silly about cast iron, was so sensible about most things that matter and he observed that for every hundred men who can write there is only one who can think, and for every hundred who can think there is only one who can *see*. John Gay can see. He has an eye which alights on all the joyful, subtle detail over which architects and designers once took such trouble. And his eye guides his lens, so that his atmospheric and often poignant photographs can show others what visual delights abound on all sides, delights moulded and made of that substance we take too much for granted.

SELECT BIBLIOGRAPHY

Raymond Lister, *Decorative Cast Ironwork in Great Britain*. London, 1960.

E. Graeme and Joan Robertson, *Cast Iron Decoration. A World Survey*. Thames & Hudson, London, 1977.

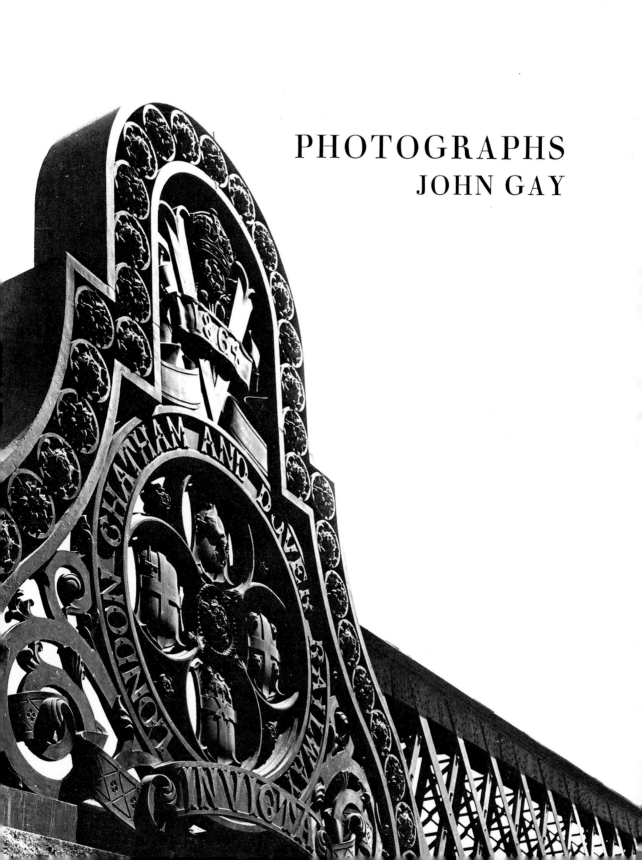

PHOTOGRAPHS
JOHN GAY

GRAND

8

11

12

14

16

24

28

34

REAT   EA   HOTE

Rail Frei

38

39

GEORGE SMITH & Co. SUN FOUNDRY GLASGOW

45

48

49

Z.D.BERRY & SON · REGENT STREET · WESTMINSTER

50

51

GOOD FRIDAY, APRIL 12th, 1974 at 7 p.

BRIGHTON & HOVE HARMONIC SOCIETY

present

MESSIAH

Soloists:
Caroline Clack   Fiona Kimms
Charles Corp   John Huw Davies
Nick Bomford (Trumpet)

STRING ORCHESTRA
(LEADER: FRANK CLIFFORD)

Organist: Basil Waymark
Conductor: Ralph Nicholson

ADMISSION   RESERVED   75p   60p   40p

60

64

77

79

LIST OF PHOTOGRAPHS